Solv-a-Crime Puzzles

SINGER MEDIA CORPORATION

EDITED BY KURT SINGER
WRITTEN BY A. C. GORDON

DOVER PUBLICATIONS, INC.
New York

Copyright

Published in Canada by General Publishing Company, Ltd., 30 Lesmill Road, Don Mills, Toronto, Ontario.

Bibliographical Note

This Dover edition, first published in 1995, is an unabridged republication of the work first published by Scholastic Book Services, New York, 1972 (as *Solv-a-Crime*). The Dover edition is newly set in type, and a brief Introduction has been added.

Library of Congress Cataloging-in-Publication Data

Gordon, A. C.
   [Solv-a-crime]
   Solv-a-crime puzzles / edited by Kurt Singer (Singer Media Corporation) ; written by A.C. Gordon.
     p.   cm. — (Dover game and puzzle activity books)
   Originally published: Solv-a-crime. New York : Scholastic Book Services, 1972. With new introd.
   ISBN 0-486-28552-9 (pbk.)
   1. Puzzles. 2. Detective and mystery stories. I. Singer, Kurt D., 1911–   II. Singer Media Corporation. III. Title. IV. Series.
GV1507.D4G67   1995
793.73 — dc20
                                 94-40593
                                     CIP

Manufactured in the United States of America
Dover Publications, Inc., 31 East 2nd Street, Mineola, N.Y. 11501

Introduction

HAVE YOU EVER wanted to be a detective? Well, now is your chance! These 47 brief mysteries will challenge your deductive skills. Read each mystery *very* carefully: there are clues cleverly hidden where you least expect them! As you go you will be matching wits with a host of devilish burglars, con men, murderers—some of them fiendishly ingenious lawbreakers!

If you are ready to give up (not even Sherlock Holmes solved *every* crime!), the solutions are printed, upside-down, after each mystery.

Contents

The Case of the Artist's Accident

"My name is Tom Randall," says the voice on the phone. "I'm a friend of Philip McLean's. There's been a horrible accident at his studio!"

Fifteen minutes later, you're looking at the body on the floor in front of an easel, next to a huge puddle of bright red paint. Over McLean's right temple is a gruesome, bloody wound.

You note the victim's immaculate clothing: powder blue sport coat, elegant maroon tie, snow-white shirt, light gray slacks, and tan shoes—even the soles are spotless. An unfinished color illustration rests on the easel.

Tom Randall begins, "I hadn't seen Phil for several months, since just before he got married. I'll tell you about this now, since you're sure to find out about it. The girl he married used to be engaged to me. There was some bad feeling between Phil and me, but it all got smoothed over."

"Suppose you tell me how this happened," you say.

"I had a sudden impulse this afternoon to pay Phil a surprise visit, to let him know I didn't bear any grudges. When I came into the studio, he was painting, his back to me. I guess he didn't hear me come in. Then when I spoke, I must have really startled him. He dropped that paint on the floor, and as he turned around quickly, he accidentally stepped into the paint, slipped, and hit his head on the corner of the easel! The blow, combined with the fact that he had a weak heart, must've done it. I called you as soon as I got over my shock. I only wonder how Betty will feel when she hears the story!"

"*Story* is right!" you snap. "I want you to tell me the truth!"

Why are you doubtful of Randall's story?

If Philip McLean had stepped in and slipped in the red paint, as Randall claimed, some of the paint would have at least been on the soles of his shoes. But they were spotless. Also, it's very unlikely that an artist who was working with paint would have been dressed the way McLean was.

1

The Case of the Banker's Letter

Keith Stratton, a young bank vice-president, has vanished from town with a huge amount of the bank's money. All efforts to find him have failed, but you have just had a phone call from Sandra Hammond. She is the girl that Stratton went with steadily at one time, until he jilted her for her "best friend," Betty Waring—as reported in all the newspapers that feature social news.

Now you are sitting in the lobby of Sandra Hammond's luxury apartment building, waiting to hear the "vital information" she has promised to give you about the missing embezzler.

Finally Sandra Hammond sweeps into the lobby through the street door. "I'm so sorry to have kept you waiting," she says. "I phoned you from Betty Waring's apartment—one of her cocktail parties."

She takes you up to her huge apartment and begins her story. "Betty Waring, I'm certain, can tell you where Keith is. During the party, I went into her bedroom to fix my make-up, and I found the first page of a letter written to her by Keith. I'm not ashamed to admit I read it—a lot of silly sentiment and not much information. That first page, however, ended in the middle of a sentence, and it seemed interesting. I'm sure if you find the second page—"

You interrupt to hand Miss Hammond a sheet of paper that you found in Stratton's apartment. "Is this Stratton's handwriting?" you ask.

Sandra stares fixedly at the paper. She shakes her head and begins fumbling in her purse. Then she searches through the drawers of a desk, coming up with a pair of glasses. She puts them on, studies the paper again, and says, "Yes, this is Keith's writing. No doubt about it."

"Miss Hammond," you say, "I suspect that this story you've been telling me is pure fiction—probably made up out of jealousy and intended to cause trouble for Betty Waring!"

Why do you suspect this?

2

You have seen that Sandra Hammond cannot read without glasses. When she returned from Betty Waring's party, she was neither wearing them nor carrying them in her purse. It would have been impossible, therefore, for her to read the letter she claimed she read in Betty's bedroom.

The Case of the Bashful Boarder

Your search for Hank Travers, a robbery suspect, has led you to a rundown boardinghouse on Beach Street. You ask Lil Cartwright, the fat, sloppy landlady, about him.

"Oh, sure—Hank has a room here," she says. "But I can tell you right now, before you start snooping—he hasn't been around for over a week."

"I'd like to look at his room," you say.

"If you can get in, it's all yours," says Lil. "Hank put a special lock on his door—he said he liked his privacy. I don't have a key for it."

Groaning with her weight and muttering about "snoopers," Lil leads you up to the third floor. She watches you test your assortment of keys in the lock.

"Wouldn't some people I know give their eyeteeth for that set of keys," she says.

The lock yields to one of the keys, and you enter the dingy room. The landlady follows you inside, casts an eye at the cheap little alarm clock ticking noisily on the dust-covered dresser, and says, "Five o'clock—I've got to get supper on the stove."

She goes downstairs, and you carefully examine the room. You fail to turn up a single clue. All you find is a crumpled cigaret package, a dirty-looking razor, an old felt hat, and two ties with grease spots.

Downstairs in the kitchen, you watch Lil for a minute, then say,

3

"I wonder if you'll tell me a little more about Hank Travers—or do I have to take you to headquarters for questioning?"

"I told you, I don't know anything about him!" she yells. "No one's been in that room since Hank left over a week ago!"

"And I say either Hank or one of his friends has been here within the last day or so!"

How do you know?

The "cheap little alarm clock ticking noisily on the . . . dresser" would not be running unless someone had wound it within the last day or two.

The Case of the Body in the Barn

You arrive at the large country home of wealthy Keith Kendall. Terry Ahern and Don Benning, the junior partners in Kendall's firm, lead you to the barn at the rear of the house. Inside, lying faceup on the floor, is Kendall's corpse, with a kitchen knife sticking out of his chest.

You dust the handle of the knife and find one set of well-defined fingerprints. Then you take prints of Ahern and Benning, and compare them with the ones on the knife.

"The only prints on the knife are yours, Ahern," you say. "But you've told me the knife comes from the kitchen in the house and that you haven't been in the kitchen all day."

"I can explain," Ahern replies. "Don and I drove here today on business. When we couldn't find Mr. Kendall in the house, we started looking for him. The estate is so large, Don and I separated. When I got to the barn, there was Mr. Kendall, with that knife in him! I started to pull the knife out—that's how my fingerprints got on it—and that's just when Don came walking in."

Don Benning says, "You can imagine my horror when I walked

4

into the barn and found Terry bent over the body—holding a knife! His face turned pale when he looked up and saw me."

"It happened as I said!" shouts Ahern. "I had no reason to—"

"How about that argument you had with him yesterday?" Benning says. "You told me afterwards that you were fed up with his constant criticism, and you were going to do something drastic about it!"

"I didn't *kill* him," Ahern mumbles. He turns to you. "Could it have been suicide?"

"No, it wasn't suicide," you say. "It was murder, and I'm taking one of you with me for questioning!"

Whom do you suspect, and why?

You suspect Don Benning. The only fingerprints on the knife were Ahern's, which leads you to believe he is innocent, and that someone wiped the handle clean after the murder and before Ahern touched it. If it had been suicide, Kendall's prints would have been on the handle too. And if Ahern had done it, he would not have been so foolish as to wipe the handle clean and then deliberately incriminate himself by putting his prints back on the handle.

The Case of the Body on the Berth

You're on a ship in the Caribbean. Because of a raging storm tossing the ship around for the past hour, you've been unable to sleep. All you can do is cling to your bed, to keep from being thrown all around your cabin.

Just as the storm is subsiding, there is a knock on your door. "Sorry to disturb you," says Raymond Shannon, the ship's First Officer. "Something terrible has happened! About an hour ago, before the storm hit us, I was hurrying along a dark passageway—and I almost tripped over a body lying there! It's Henry Kruger, the millionaire—with a bullet in his forehead."

5

"Why did it take you an hour to report it?" you ask.

"There was so much to do—with the storm coming up," he replies. "I guess I should have left him where I found him, but I wasn't thinking very clearly.

"I carried him into an empty cabin, put him on a berth, and locked the door. I didn't have time to tell anyone. I still haven't even told the Captain. Would you mind coming with me and looking at the body?"

You go with him until he stops at a door and unlocks it. Inside, you see the body lying on the berth, faceup, the hands resting on the body as though in sleep, but with a bullet hole in the forehead. There are spots of blood on the carpet.

You turn to Shannon. "Does anyone else have access to this cabin?"

"There are a couple of keys in the Captain's quarters, but I know they're still there. I have a master key to all the cabins, the only one we have, and that's what I used to open this cabin."

"I think you also have a master talent for lying!" you say. "You'd better tell me the truth."

Why do you doubt Shannon's story?

You remember how you had to cling to your bed while the ship was tossing in the storm. Yet, according to Shannon, the body had lain on the berth throughout the storm, hands resting undisturbed and all. Surely it would have been thrown off the berth during the storm.

The Case of the Borrowed Baby

You drive to one of the city's fanciest addresses in response to a phone call about a kidnapping. You ring and the door is opened by a distraught-looking housemaid. "Thank goodness, you're here!" she cries.

"Mr. and Mrs. Harding are away for the weekend," she goes on.

6

"I was left in charge of Jerry. He's two years old. I left him playing in his room with all his toys, and went downstairs to the kitchen. Then I thought I heard some footsteps upstairs, so I rushed up to the baby's room—and there a man was climbing out the window with Jerry in his arms! I just stood there in a state of shock. Then I screamed and ran to the window.

"I saw the man jump off the ladder when he was 10 feet from the ground—with the baby! He almost dropped Jerry when he landed! Then he ran to a black car, tossed the baby in, and raced away." She bursts into sobs.

You look at the crumpled blankets on the baby's bed, and the spilled baby powder all over the floor. A set of a large man's footprints in the powder lead from the bed to the open window. Everything else in the room is neat and orderly.

You go outside the house and around to where the ladder leans against the house, under the baby's window. There are a few faint footprints in the soft dirt around the foot of the ladder, but nothing else of any interest, on the ground or on the ladder.

The maid joins you and shows you a piece of paper she says was in the mailbox. You read: "Your baby will come back alive for $50,000. You'll hear from us soon."

"Do you think we should phone Mr. and Mrs. Harding?" she asks.

"By all means," you say. "As soon as you tell me where the baby is!"

Why do you suspect the maid?

First, because you found only a man's footprints in the powder on the floor. If the maid rushed over to the window as she said, *her* footprints would have been there too. Also, you found no traces of powder on the rungs of the ladder; and, on the ground below, you found only faint footprints—yet, if the man had jumped from the ladder while 10 feet off the ground, as she said, there would have been deep impressions in the soft dirt. Finally, the maid said she had left the baby playing with toys in his room—but, except for the powder and messy blankets, the room was all in order.

The Case of the Bruised Blonde

You arrive at Debby Dell's apartment 15 minutes after she phones you. Whoever beat her up was thorough: black eye swollen shut, lips puffy and cut, and face all bruised.

"I couldn't see who it was, it happened so quick!" she exclaims. "When I came home, I just opened the door and got hit over the head, from behind. In a blur, I saw a guy in a mask standing over me. He beat me till I passed out. When I came to, I called you."

"Any idea who might have done it, Miss Dell?" you ask.

She thinks a moment. "Well, my ex-boyfriend, Jerry Whitman, is pretty sore. We had a big fight last night, and we broke up. For good. I even had my phone number changed this morning to an unlisted one, so the creep can't bug me on the phone. But he wouldn't have done something like this to me!"

"Any other ideas?"

"Maybe one of Marty Bruno's muscle men. Marty runs the Red Line Café over in the North End. I dropped two hundred bucks at one of his dice tables a few weeks ago. I haven't been able to pay up. Maybe this was a warning."

The ringing of the phone interrupts her. She picks it up, and you hear her say, "Look, I told you last night, it's no go! And that's final!" She slams the phone down. "That was Jerry. He won't take no for an answer."

"I think there are some answers he can give *me*," you say. "I'm going to pay him a little visit right now!"

Why do you suspect Jerry Whitman?

Debby told you that her phone number was changed to an unlisted one that morning. The only way that Jerry could have learned her new number was by seeing it printed on the phone itself—in Debby's apartment that day.

The Case of the Bullet in the Broker

The body of Ralph Hodge, stockbroker, lies on the carpet in his office with a bullet hole in his back.

"It was self-defense," says his young clerk, Dick Richter. "We were struggling for the gun." He points to a .45 on the floor near the corpse. "We were wrestling face-to-face, with the gun between us, when it went off! He was dead before he hit the floor!" Richter shudders. "Everyone knows about his violent temper, but I never thought he'd try to use a gun on me!"

"Let's have the whole story," you say.

"Well, several times this week, Mr. Hodge had called me on the carpet, saying I was taking too much credit for some deals we were putting through. He said it was *his* business, built on *his* name. That sort of thing. He accused me of trying to take over and referred to me sarcastically as 'a regular boy wonder.' "

"What happened today?" you ask.

"He was worse than ever. He called me in here and started in on me again. I walked away from him, to avoid saying something I might later regret. I was standing at the window, letting the rays of the sun warm my face, trying to relax and come up with the right arguments. Then I saw his reflection in the window! He was coming up behind me with that gun in his hand! I wheeled around and struggled with him. I grabbed his gun hand and—well, you heard the rest."

"Yes, I heard it," you say, "but I don't believe it!"

Why are you suspicious of Richter's story?

First, if the sun had been shining through the window on his face, as he stated, he could not have seen any reflection on the glass from behind him. Second, if he and his boss had been struggling face-to-face when the gun went off, how did the victim get shot in the back?

The Case of the Bludgeoned Bachelor

Peter Norris, a wealthy old bachelor, is dead at his desk in his home. The back of his head is smashed and bloody. Behind him is the weapon—a fireplace poker covered with bloodstains.

Norris lived with his three nieces—Catherine, Anne, and Denise Denton.

"I won't pretend to mourn," says Catherine. "He was stingy and bad-tempered. All the same, he didn't deserve this!"

"Nothing we did ever pleased him," chimes in Anne. "He was always criticizing the way I dress, even these high-heeled shoes. He complained about the noise they made—he said he could even hear them when I walked down the street. Only this afternoon, when I walked across the tiled floor toward his desk, he flew into a rage because of the noise."

Denise is nervously toying with her jangly, noisy charm bracelet. "I was reading in my room this afternoon when I heard Catherine scream. Anne and I got here at the same time, and—oh, it's so awful!"

"I've checked the fireplaces in all the rooms," you say, "and the poker from your room is missing, Denise!"

"I don't understand!" she cries. "I didn't know it was gone!"

"She quarreled with Uncle Peter just this morning," says Catherine.

"Neither of you others heard anything suspicious this afternoon until Catherine screamed?" you ask. Anne and Denise shake their heads.

"I suspect one of you murdered your uncle," you say. "And I think I know which one."

Whom do you suspect, and why?

Catherine. Peter Norris must have had good hearing, since Anne said he claimed to have heard her high heels in the street. Since the murderer must have caught him unawares from behind, he would have heard Anne's shoes or Denise's charm bracelet. Furthermore, Catherine's pointing out Denise's quarrel with Norris, coupled with the use of Denise's poker, is very suspicious.

The Case of the Burgled Businessman

You are called to the home of businessman Henry Harris. "I'm very upset," he says. "Not just because of the stolen money—that's insured—but because of who the logical suspects are."

"Tell me about it," you say.

"Well," Harris says, "when I went to my office this morning, I had left some important papers in my safe here at home. I sent Alice Geiger, my secretary, to fetch them. Half an hour later, she phoned to say she'd found the safe open and papers all over the study! I hurried home, and found that the cash in the safe was missing—more than $3,000! The only people who knew the combination were Miss Geiger, my housekeeper, Mrs. Kearns, and Tucker, my butler."

You examine the safe, the study door, the desk, and the phone for fingerprints, but you find none. You call the three suspects into the room.

Alice Geiger is the first. "I was shocked when I came into the study and saw the safe open and the papers all over the floor. I grabbed the phone and called Mr. Harris. Then I called the butler and the housekeeper in."

Mrs. Kearns says, "I was cleaning the bedrooms, and I didn't know Miss Geiger was in the house until I heard her voice. I thought no one had been in the study this morning besides Mr. Harris."

"I let Miss Geiger in the front door," says Tucker. "Then I was in the kitchen when I heard her cry out, about ten minutes later."

"Has anyone touched anything in the room since the theft was discovered?" you ask.

They all shake their heads.

Then you point your finger dramatically and say, "You—are the guilty one!"

Who is your suspect, and why?

Alice Geiger. In her eagerness to remove incriminating finger-prints, she wiped clean not only the safe, the study door, and the desk, but even the telephone. Her prints could have innocently been on all these things, especially on the phone—which she used to call Mr. Harris!

The Case of the Burnt-Out Store

"Please come at once!" says a hoarse voice over the telephone. "This is Joseph Welton. I own a store at 624 Central Avenue. A thief has burned it down—I caught him in the act. I have him here ready for you!"

You hurry to Central Avenue, where the firemen are putting out the last of the flames. The store is practically demolished. A wild-eyed man rushes up to you—Joseph Welton.

"The firebug is tied up in the shed behind the store," he says. "I came back to the store tonight to do my bookkeeping. As I unlocked the door, I saw one side of the store in flames. Then, on the other side, I saw this bum bending over the cash register, scooping out the money and stuffing it into his pockets. So I snuck up and knocked him out with a punch on the jaw. Then I dragged him out of the store and pulled the fire alarm. I tied him up and dragged him to the shed."

You follow Welton to the shed, where you see the seedy-looking man, still unconscious on the floor. You note the ugly gash over his right temple as you bend over him to go through his pockets, looking for some identification. The pockets are empty.

"Do you have any idea who he is?" you ask Welton.

"No, I've never seen him before."

"Tell me," you ask, "do you have adequate fire insurance?"

"Oh, yes."

"You know, Welton," you say, "I think you set fire to the store yourself—so you could collect that insurance money!"

Why do you think that?

Welton said he caught the "intruder" as he was putting money from the cash register into his pockets. Yet you found nothing in the unconscious man's pockets—and Welton said nothing about recovering his money. Furthermore, there was a gash over the man's temple, although Welton said he knocked him out with a punch on the jaw. This leads you to suspect Welton of setting up an innocent down-and-outer as a pigeon for the law.

The Case of the Captive Clerk

As you are walking along early one morning, you are hailed by your friend Joe Benson, who is unlocking the door of his clothing store. He invites you in for a chat.

As you accompany him into the office at the rear of the store, you see one of Benson's sales clerks, Miles Burnett, sitting with his hands and feet tied to a chair and a handkerchief knotted tightly over his mouth.

Even more astounding, the door of the safe is wide open and the safe is practically empty. The floor of the office is covered with papers, and the chair in which Burnett is squirming rests on some of the papers.

After you and Benson have untied Burnett, he blurts out his story. "I arrived at the store at the usual time this morning. I had just opened the safe when a voice behind me said, 'This is a stick-up.' Another voice said, 'Don't move or make a sound.' "

"Did you get a look at them?" you ask.

"Well, over my shoulder—it was two men with nylon hose pulled down over their faces. One of them was holding a gun. The other one pushed me into that chair and tied and gagged me. Then they went through the safe, throwing papers all over the office until they got to the cash."

"How long had they been gone before we came into the store?" Joe Benson asks.

"Only about five minutes," Burnett says. "I was still almost paralyzed when I heard you coming in. They had warned me not to move or try to get loose—but I couldn't have moved an inch if I'd tried."

"Well," you say, "I think you'll be moving now—with me to headquarters. You've told us a good story—but not good enough!"

Why do you think Burnett had something to do with the theft?

According to Burnett, the thieves did not loot the safe until they had tied Burnett to the chair. Yet the chair in which he was tied so securely was resting *on top of* some of the papers the thieves were supposed to have tossed out of the safe—and Burnett claimed he was too paralyzed to move after the thieves had left.

The Case of Cody's Corpse

Matthew Cody, realtor, was stabbed to death late this evening, and $700 was taken from the safe in his office.

At Cody's downtown office you find Bill Frye, Cody's partner, talking to Jake Kessel, the building janitor, in the corridor outside the office. You go inside.

The body is leaning back in the swivel chair behind the desk, facing the door you have just entered. When you're quite near the

14

dead man, you see the switchblade knife stuck between his shoulderblades, the handle protruding over the back of the chair.

You ask Kessel what happened.

"I was carrying some trash along the corridor," he says. "I saw through the glass door that the lights in here were still on. I thought that was funny—it was after ten. So I opened the door, stuck my head in, and almost swallowed my cigar! There he was, leaning back in his chair, with that awful look on his face, and that knife stuck in him! So I ran like the devil down that corridor, to the phone, and I ran right into Mr. Frye, who was just coming in. I told him all about it."

You turn to Bill Frye. "About an hour ago," he says, "I got a phone call from Matt, here at the office. He said he was working late, and he asked if I could get here for some business matters that couldn't wait. When I got here, I ran into Jake, and he told me what happened."

"Has either of you touched anything in here since you discovered the body?" you ask.

Both reply in the negative. Your eyes fix on one of them, and you say, "Part of your story is a lie!"

To whom have you spoken, and why?

Jake the janitor. He said that as soon as he opened the door, he saw the knife in Cody's back. This was impossible, since Cody was facing the door in a leaning-back position.

The Case of the Corpse in the Cabin

You're checking out the cabin: first, the front room: two unmade beds on one side, a table heaped with dirty dishes on the other. When you get to the kitchen, you see the bloody body of Jed Higgins sprawled on the floor behind the table, a knife sticking out of his chest.

Joe Anderson, who phoned you about this, appears in the

doorway. "Why would anyone want to kill poor old Jed? He was such a great guy. He and I were a great team in our business. But it couldn't have been money the killer was after. That was the first thing I thought of—but Jed's wallet is still in his hip pocket, untouched."

"What happened?" you ask.

"We came here for a weekend of fishing. This morning Jed wasn't feeling well, so he stayed in bed. I spent about three hours out on the lake in our boat, and came back about noon. I opened the front door—and I saw him lying there, covered with blood! I couldn't even come into the cabin, I was so sick and upset! Finally, though, I drove into town to phone you, and I've stayed outside waiting for you."

You stay at the door of the cabin for a while. Suddenly you wheel around and stalk back into the kitchen. You take one more look at the body, hidden behind the table.

Finally you say, "Anderson, I knew something was fishy around here—and it was you! You're under suspicion of murder!"

Why do you suspect Anderson?

Anderson said that when he returned to the cabin, he opened the front door and immediately saw his partner's body. He could not have seen the body from the front door, since it was hidden behind the table, in the kitchen. He also said that he never entered the cabin; how, then, could he know the dead man's wallet was untouched?

The Case of the Councilman's Corpse

Twelve noon downtown is noisy and hectic. No one notices anything. Like everyone else, you are busy with your own thoughts today. But even downtown at noon, some things *do* get noticed. Like a body falling out of a 32nd-floor window.

It lands at your feet. You step aside, then narrowly miss being conked on the head by a heavy leather briefcase that lands a few feet from the body.

"It's Fred Fuller, the city councilman!" someone shrieks.

As an ambulance jolts to a stop, you dash into the building the body left so precipitously, and start asking questions. You learn that Fred Fuller took the elevator to the 32nd floor. You take the same elevator to the same stop: Carter and Stuart, Stockbrokers.

Carter says, "Fuller was our best client. We were reviewing his investments. We finished our talk, and he was preparing to leave. He walked over to the window, commenting on the fine view. Then, before I knew what was happening, he leaned out too far—he must have gotten dizzy or something—lost his balance, gave out a horrible scream—and fell!"

Stuart says, "I was just leaving the room when he screamed. I wheeled around—but he was gone, his briefcase still clutched in his hand! Ghastly!" He shudders.

"Ghastly, I agree," you say. "But I mean the story you two concocted. I'm taking you both in for questioning! This was no accident—this was murder!"

How do you know it was murder?

Fuller's briefcase landed several seconds *after* his body, and a few feet from it. If he had been holding the briefcase and hadn't let go of it in the fall, it would have landed at the same time he did. And Stuart stated that he did not see the actual fall, yet referred to the briefcase clutched in Fuller's hand. Your conclusion is that Fuller was pushed out the window and his briefcase thrown after him.

The Case of the Counterfeit Cousin

At the Tulip Tree Café you run into a young friend, Dick Turner. Dick introduces you to another man of about the same age, Malcolm Morley.

"Malcolm is a long-lost cousin of mine," Dick says. "We haven't seen each other for 15 years—ever since he left home to join the merchant marine. He's first mate of his ship now, and it was only after a long search and many ads in the newspapers that our lawyers managed to trace his whereabouts."

"Lawyers?" you ask.

"Yes—to tell him that Uncle Harry died a couple of months ago, and that Malcolm and I are his only heirs."

"It's good to be home again," Morley says. "I ran across the ad over in England just after we docked our boat. So I caught another boat as soon as I could, heading back for the States. We really had a stormy time of it crossing over."

"How did you get that ugly bruise on the side of your head?" you ask.

"We were rolling around really hard during the storm, and I was going from the front of the boat back to the kitchen to grab myself a cup of coffee. The granddaddy of all waves came at us. Before I could catch hold of anything, it hit us. I was thrown hard against the wall—almost knocked me out."

Dick Turner sets down his glass, smiles broadly, and says, "Well, we're happy to have Malcolm home again. Now we can get down to the business of settling up Uncle Harry's estate."

"I'm not so sure you want to settle up that estate yet," you say. "I doubt very much that this man is your cousin, Malcolm Morley!"

Why do you suspect the identity of the man who says he is Malcolm Morley?

It is unlikely that a man who has spent over 15 years at sea would call his ship a *boat*. Nor would he speak of the *front*, *kitchen*, or *wall*. A sailor would say: *forward*, *galley*, and *bulkhead*.

The Case of the Dead Dancer

You arrive at the lake shore, where the body was found in the bushes. You deduce that she was taken by surprise and strangled from behind. After you take off her dark glasses and scarf, you see that she was a very attractive blonde. In her purse you find four one-dollar bills, a silver lighter with the initials "R.L." and a driver's license made out to Rita Lang, age 22.

Later you learn that she was a chorus girl in a local nightclub. The evening newspaper carries the story, featuring a picture of Rita in one of her dance costumes. The sheriff's office has found that Tommy Griffin, a local playboy, was seen boating on the lake the afternoon of the murder.

You question Griffin. "I figured you'd be after me," Griffin says, with a smile. "I knew I'd been seen on the lake. That was what popped in my mind when I saw the girl's picture in the paper. I recognized her at once—the same girl I saw walking along the shore with her boyfriend—or friend. He was a thin man in a dark green suit. They seemed to be arguing, because I saw him grab her shoulders and shake her violently!"

"How far away were you?" you ask.

Tommy thinks for a moment. "Oh, I'd say at least 250 yards or so. I didn't hang around watching—I mind my own business. It wasn't till I saw the papers that I knew what had happened! Such a pretty girl, too." He shakes his head mournfully.

"Did you ever meet or see Rita Lang before?" you ask.

"No," Griffin says.

"I don't think you're telling the truth!" you say. "I'm holding you on suspicion of murder."

Why do you suspect Griffin?

Tommy Griffin said he had never met or seen Rita Lang before. Nevertheless, he recognized her picture in the paper as the girl he had supposedly seen from 250 yards away—and wearing dark glasses and a scarf!

19

The Case of Death at the Staircase

"I've had you brought in for questioning regarding the murder of Tom Garrison," you say to Bill Manning. You have just returned from the scene of the crime. Garrison's body was found at the bottom of some newly built stairs in the warehouse where he worked, and a worker said he had seen a man who "looked like Manning" running out of the building.

A huge wound in the side of Garrison's skull showed the cause of his death. Some spatters of blood on the stairs have led you to believe he might have fallen on the stairs. All the same, you sent for Manning as soon as you returned from the warehouse.

"I'll admit I had good reason to hate Garrison," Manning growls. "But I didn't club him over the head—even if he did steal my girl. Anyway, how do you know he was murdered? He could have slipped down those new stairs they built at the warehouse. They're slippery enough."

You ask, "When did you work at the warehouse with Garrison?"

"Until about two years ago. They're a skinflint outfit and I quit—haven't been back there since."

"How long has it been since you last saw Garrison?" you ask.

"The last time I saw him was two weeks ago. I had a date with my steady girl—or so I thought. When I got to her apartment—half an hour early—she and Garrison were sneaking out together. We had a big argument. And that was the last time I saw him—or my girl."

"I think you're lying to me," you say. "I think you saw Tom Garrison about an hour ago—long enough to kill him!"

Why do you think Bill Manning is a murderer?

Although you haven't mentioned the manner of Garrison's death, Manning showed that he knew it was caused by a head wound when he said, "I didn't club him over the head." He also knew the body was found near some stairs. Furthermore, if he hadn't been in the warehouse for two years, how did he know about the newly built stairs?

The Case of the Ex-Athlete's End

The 6-foot-7-inch body of Pat Harding, former basketball star and rising young politician, lies sprawled on the sidewalk. The bullet that killed him entered the top of his shoulder and ended up in his heart.

Down at headquarters, Lt. Larkin fills you in on a suspect: "A couple of seconds after the shot was fired, one of our men saw this guy break through the crowd and race down the street—so he nabbed him. The guy says his name's Vickers and he used to be a jockey. Of course, he says he doesn't know a thing about the murder."

"Right!" Vickers says. "Just hanging around there doesn't mean I did anything!"

"Then why were you running away?" you ask.

"I just don't like looking at stiffs!"

Vickers mops his face with a monogrammed handkerchief and lights a cigaret. You look him over: well-cut sport coat, expensive tie, imported shoes. For his size (about 5 feet 5) he cuts quite a figure.

"Anything else to say?" you ask.

"Nothing. Nothing. I heard the shot, just like everybody else. First I thought it was a car backfiring—then I saw him there on the sidewalk. Like I said, I don't cotton to stiffs, so I took off!"

"You'll have to let him go, Lieutenant," you say to Larkin. "He couldn't have shot Harding!"

What makes you think so?

The downward course of the bullet that killed Harding. The five-five Vickers could not have fired a bullet into the shoulder of a 6'7" man, with the bullet going downward into the heart.

The Case of the Falling Moon

It is a brutally cold day. You get to the office building of wealthy stockbroker Martin Moon just as the ambulance is pulling away. Moon's body landed on the sidewalk after falling from a window eight floors up.

His office is in a turmoil—two girls in a corner of the outer office crying hysterically, three men pacing back and forth. One of the men says, "I'm Milton Kearns, a junior partner here. We were all in the outer office when we heard him scream. I rushed into Mr. Moon's office, but it was too late! That man over there, Bill Franklin, was with Mr. Moon and saw him jump."

Bill Franklin walks over to you. "I was an employee here, until a year ago, when Mr. Moon and I had a little disagreement. I dropped in today to see if there was a chance of my coming back to work here."

"What happened?" you ask.

"Well, he started to walk around the office. He seemed worried about something. Just as he got near the open window, he turned toward it. Then—I don't know if he jumped or lost his balance!" He shakes his head.

You step into Moon's office with Milton Kearns. The room is uncomfortably warm, because of two electric heaters in the corners. Kearns comments, "Mr. Moon was not a healthy man, and he always complained of the cold. He kept his office in here like an oven. And he resented anyone's suggestion of ventilation or fresh air."

"Mr. Moon neither committed suicide nor had an accident," you say to Kearns. "I'll have to ask Bill Franklin some more questions!"

Why do you suspect Franklin?

You can't understand why the window was open at the time of the "accident." Kearns told you that Moon hated fresh air. And if he kept two heaters going in his office, he wouldn't have had the window open.

22

The Case of the Fishing Politician

An outspoken politician named Fred Turner was murdered several days ago, shot in cold blood as he mowed his front lawn. Finally, only one suspect remains: Harvey Haynes, another active politician, well-known as a bitter opponent of Turner's.

Backed by a search warrant, you have gone through Haynes' apartment and found a gun, tucked in the back of a dresser drawer under a pile of shirts. A test has revealed that it is the gun that killed Turner.

Now you bring Haynes in for questioning. "You can't prove I was the one who did the killing," he says. "I found the gun just a couple of days ago—in the north end of the lake in County Park—while I was fishing."

"You found it in the water?" you ask.

"Yeah, I was in a small rented boat—fishing, as I told you. I was rowing when I spotted something shining through the water on the bottom of the lake. It's only about two or three feet deep there. So I fished down into the water with a hook and line, and I hooked the gun and brought it up. I took it home, cleaned it up, and put it away. I didn't figure on anyone searching my flat and trying to pin a murder rap on me."

"What day did you say you found this gun?" you ask.

"I said a couple of days ago." Haynes pauses to think. "It was Tuesday afternoon."

"Tuesday afternoon?" you ask. "Do you mean you were out fishing on the lake in the steady rainfall we had all that afternoon?"

"Oh, sure," he says casually. "A little rain doesn't bother me."

"Maybe this will bother you," you say. "You're under suspicion of murdering Fred Turner!"

Why do you doubt Haynes' story?

A steady rainfall on the surface of the lake would have made it impossible for Haynes to see the gun "shining through the water on the bottom of the lake."

The Case of the Frisky Dog

A young housewife, Mrs. Betty Hargrave, has phoned you. She is terribly distressed by the fact that Henry Courtenay, a neighbor in her apartment building, has threatened to sue her.

"Our eight-year-old son, Tommy," she says, "was outside playing with our little Scottish terrier, Dougall. He's a dear little dog, and quite harmless. Well, Mr. Courtenay came along and Dougall playfully jumped against Mr. Courtenay. Mr. Courtenay hates dogs, so he kicked Dougall away, and Tommy held him while Mr. Courtenay got into his car and drove away."

"Then what?" you ask.

"I just had a call from Mr. Courtenay. He said he's at Community Hospital receiving emergency treatment—for a wound on his leg, where the dog bit him! He said he plans to sue us for plenty."

After you assure Mrs. Hargrave that you'll investigate the matter, you hurry over to the hospital. You find sour-faced Henry Courtenay in an examining room, preparing to leave. You ask the doctor if you may examine the wound.

The doctor draws up the sharply creased, spotlessly clean leg of Courtenay's light gray trousers. He carefully removes the bandage, revealing freshly cauterized marks on the right calf.

You ask the doctor, "Are you sure these are a dog's tooth marks?"

The doctor replies, "They look like it, but I wouldn't swear to it."

Then you ask Courtenay, "Did you come here immediately after the incident in front of your apartment building?"

"You bet I did!" he says. "You can't take a chance with a dog bite."

"I think you're taking chances," you say, "with a foolish attempt to frame a charge against the Hargraves. I think you inflicted that wound on your leg yourself—maybe with a fork—to look like tooth marks. In any event, I'm sure the Hargraves' dog did not bite you!"

What has led you to this conclusion?

Courtenay told you he drove directly to the hospital from the scene of the incident—so he could not have changed his clothes. Yet despite the fact that the wound is in the calf of his leg, there are no tooth marks or punctures in the leg of his trousers.

The Case of the Gas-Filled Study

When you arrive at the home of millionaire Bedford Grant, his frantic housekeeper lets you in.

"Something terrible has happened—I'm sure of it!" she cries. "There's a smell of gas coming from Mr. Grant's study. I pounded on the door, but I couldn't get any answer—and it's locked. Please hurry—it's this way."

You run through the house after the woman, as she leads you to the door of Grant's study. You try several of the keys you have brought, until one of them opens the lock. The door is hard to push open, because a small scatter rug has been wedged under the bottom crack from inside the room.

You rush across the gas-filled room to unlock the window and push it open. Clumps of cotton have been stuffed into the cracks around the window.

The housekeeper squeezes through the partly opened door and screams when she sees Grant's lifeless body. He is sprawled in a leather-covered chair, with a black scarf knotted tightly around his neck. After turning off the gas, which is whistling loudly from a pipe in the fireplace, you find a note on the desk. It reads: "Frank Anderson is the man to arrest for my murder."

You ask the housekeeper, "Who is Frank Anderson?"

"Oh," she says, "he's that gambler. He came into town a few days ago. I remember Mr. Grant saying that Anderson cheated him in a poker game. Mr. Grant swore he would get even. He had his share of bad temper—but I never saw him so worked up as he was after that poker game!"

She looks at the note and asks, "Do you think maybe Anderson heard about Mr. Grant's threats—and then he came here . . . ?"

"No," you say. "Anderson definitely didn't kill Mr. Grant."

Why are you sure of that?

The window was locked, and a killer could not have locked the door from the outside and still have left a rug stuffed under it from the inside. Mr. Grant's death was a case of suicide, with a mad attempt on his part to pin a murder charge on the man he hated.

The Case of the Gentle Jewel Thief

Inspector George Ramsey of Scotland Yard is telling you of his Atlantic crossing and his success in apprehending Brenda Gibson, international jewel thief.

"Our voyage had nearly ended," begins George, "and I was beginning to lose hope of catching her with the goods—although I was positive she had the diamonds in her possession. We were approaching the Statue of Liberty. I stood at the rail watching her. How attractive she looked, elegantly dressed, waving an elaborately long cigaret holder to point out interesting landmarks to the other passengers. Not a bit like one's notion of a jewel thief."

"She sounds lovely, George," you say. "What about the diamonds?"

"Yes. I knew I had to find them before we docked. If she got past your customs officials, all would be lost.

"Luckily I had become acquainted with her on board. We had had cocktails and danced together several times. In view of this, I told her how much I had enjoyed her company, and asked if I might have her New York telephone number.

"She agreed very sweetly and rummaged in her purse for her card. I thought at the time that she must be quite nervous, judging from the heavy nicotine stains on her fingers. And then, just as she found her card and gave it to me with a charming smile, it came to me—I knew where she was hiding the jewels! And I was right!"

Where did the Inspector find the stolen diamonds?

Inside that "elaborately long cigaret holder," Brenda had nicotine-stained fingers, indicating that she usually smoked without a holder—hence the inspector's conclusion that the holder was a prop to conceal the jewels.

The Case of Hit and Run

Mrs. John Hill was hit and killed by a speeding car around 8:40 last night. Two witnesses agreed that the car barely slowed down after striking the victim.

Just after midnight, the car was found—abandoned on a vacant lot, with bloodstains and fragments of clothing (that matched Mrs. Hill's) on its front bumper. The same car was reported stolen by its owner, Thomas Tracy, in a phone call to the police last night.

Tracy said he left his car parked with the ignition key in it, while he went into his neighborhood drugstore for cigarets. When he went outside, he discovered that his car was missing, so he hurried back into the store and phoned the police.

To check his story, you drive to the drugstore, a small establishment with a sign on the door saying: "Open Daily—9:00 to 9:00." You question the owner, Malcolm McGregor, who confirms Tracy's visit last night.

"Yes," McGregor says, "Tom came in just at closing time. He bought some cigarets, and we exchanged a few friendly words. Then he went to the phone booth and made a call."

"In that order?" you ask.

"That's right. Then he left."

You return to your office to question Tracy. He exclaims, "I hope you're able to track down that guy who used my car to kill that poor woman! You can imagine how shook up I was this morning when I learned about the accident."

"Get ready to be 'shook up' some more," you say. "You're our number-one suspect as the driver who killed Mrs. Hill!"

Why do you suspect Thomas Tracy?

The victim was hit around 8:40. But Tracy didn't report his car stolen until just before 9:00, when McGregor was closing his store. Furthermore, Tracy told you he discovered the "theft" after leaving the store, then returned to the store to make his phone call—but the druggist told you he made the call *before* leaving the store.

The Case of the Homicidal Hunter

Sheriff Henderson is on the phone. "Hunting accident. Peculiar kind of hunting, too. With bows and arrows. One of the hunters ended up as the bull's-eye. I think it was murder. I'll pick you up in 10 minutes." The sheriff never wastes words.

You drive with him up a mountain road until a forest ranger flags you down. The ranger leads you through dense undergrowth to a clearing where three somber-looking men are standing. Your eyes follow theirs—and you see a man's body pinned flat against a pine tree by an arrow, the shaft protruding horizontally from his bloodstained chest.

One of the hunters blurts out, "My name is Arlen. I was down the slope, stalking some game, when I heard Tom here cry out! I struggled up the hill and I found him pinned to that tree by that arrow! It was too late to do anything."

Ed Henson was the second. "I was closest to Tom, I guess—on the other side of this clearing. But my back was toward him, and I was about to make my way to higher ground. Then I heard the arrow whistle by me from up there—and then I heard Tom crying out in pain."

"Oh, no, you don't!" cries the third man, Vernon Lane. "That's a barefaced lie, and you know it! You're trying to pin this murder on me! I was up that slope, all right, but I didn't shoot that arrow!"

Then you say, "If all of you are telling the truth about your whereabouts at the time of the killing, one of you has practically confessed."

Whom do you suspect, and why?

The suspect is Ed Henson. The clue is the horizontal position of the arrow, since he was the only one standing on the same level with the victim at the time of the murder.

The Case of the Landscape Larceny

Joshua Herman, the director of the local art museum, has come to ask your advice. "In addition to supervising the museum's collections," he says, "I have been building my own collection of landscape paintings. There were eight of them stored in the cabinet in my private office. No one could have known about these paintings. If I may say so, they were excellent landscapes, and I was very proud of them. Then I discovered this morning that they had been stolen!"

"Who has access to this cabinet?" you ask.

"Only the other three members of the museum's board of directors. I'm sure one of them must have come across the paintings rolled up in a corner of the cabinet and made off with them. I'd appreciate your attending our board meeting this afternoon when I bring up the subject of the theft."

That afternoon, at the board meeting, Joshua Herman introduces you as "a good friend," but does not say why you are there. You meet the members of the board: stern-looking Arnold Welch, tight-lipped Mary Hawkins, and well-dressed David Mann.

"I'm sorry to say," Herman begins, "that there's been a theft—some artwork from the cabinet in my office—things I spent a lot of time and money acquiring for my personal collection at home."

Mary Hawkins breaks in, "Maybe you shouldn't have spent so much time on personal business."

"This was done perfectly legitimately," Herman says, "on my own time."

Arnold Welch says, "I agree with Mary. If you had collected those landscapes for the museum, instead of for yourself, this wouldn't have happened."

David Mann puts in, "Well, if you're suggesting that one of us had something to do with this, you can rule me out. I haven't been near the museum since our last meeting three weeks ago."

After the board meeting is adjourned, you say to Joshua Herman, "I have reason to suspect one of the three."

Whom do you suspect, and why?

Arnold Welch is the suspect. Although Herman never mentioned what kind of "artwork" had been stolen, Welch spoke knowingly of "landscapes."

The Case of the Lethal Lemonade

Wilbur Martin, elderly millionaire, lies dead on his bed. His face is gruesome; it must have been a horrible death.

Using a handkerchief, you pick up the half-empty glass of lemonade and the large pitcher that sit on the night table next to the bed. Your nostrils detect the unmistakable odor of the deadly poison that made Wilbur Martin a corpse.

Tommy Martin is Wilbur's young nephew. "There's an open package of insecticide on the window sill. He must have mixed it into his drink," he says. "It wasn't in sight when I brought Uncle Will his lemonade tonight. He liked to read in bed every night till about 10, and he always liked a pitcher of lemonade."

"Who brought it to him?" you ask.

"Usually his housekeeper—but this is her night out, so I did it for him. If I had any idea he was going to do this. . . ."

Wilbur Martin was a big name in the business world. "Was he troubled about anything lately?" you ask. "Business matters, perhaps?"

"Oh, no. Nothing wrong in his business concerns," Tommy says.

You take a look at the body again, and at the pitcher and glass on the table. Then you walk across the room to the window sill. There it is, the insecticide package, very much open and very deadly.

"I can't understand why Uncle Will would do this!" Tommy says.

"I don't think he did!" you say. "I'm taking you to headquarters for further questioning."

Why do you suspect Tommy Martin of murdering his uncle?

Someone planning to take poison would not usually mix up a whole batch in a pitcher; he would put it only in the glass he is going to drink from. Also, it is odd that the poison is on the window sill, far from the pitcher and glass. Tommy Martin's eagerness to point out the location of the poison is also suspicious.

The Case of the Maritime Murder

The small steamer you are sailing on is being rocked and tossed by a heavy storm. Suddenly a shot rings out. You hurry out to the companionway and find the steward bending over the body of millionaire Amos Potter. He has been shot through the head.

You and the captain of the ship begin checking the whereabouts of all passengers, beginning with those who were closest to the scene of the shooting. The first person you question is the victim's secretary, a tall, thin man named Philip Demarest.

"When I heard the shot," Demarest says, "I was in my stateroom writing a letter."

"May I see the letter?" you ask.

When Demarest hands over the letter, you note the small, beautiful, precise handwriting. The letter is on the ship's stationery, and is addressed to a woman named Anne.

The next stateroom is occupied by Clifford Larkin, who is extremely nervous about being questioned. He tells you that about 15 minutes before the shot was fired, he became worried about the storm and had gone to the ship's lounge for a drink. He was on his way back to his stateroom when he heard the shot.

After you and the captain have determined that there were no other passengers or crew members close by at the time of the shooting, you go back to one of the first two men and say to him: "There's something about your story that has aroused my suspicions, and I'm afraid we'll have to question you more intensively."

Whom do you suspect, and why?

Philip Demarest. You are suspicious because of the small, beautiful, precise handwriting on the letter he claimed he was writing at the time of the murder. During the storm, which was rocking the ship so badly, this kind of handwriting would have been impossible.

The Case of the Missing Money

Midnight finds you ringing Bob Traynor's doorbell. When he opens the door, you quickly size him up: young, tall and thin, pale complexion, with the shadow of a very heavy beard.

"The money!" he exclaims. "It's all gone! All the cash I collected tonight—almost $2,000! I work for the All-Heart Loan Company. Tonight I made a lot of personal calls on some of our slow-paying accounts. Very successful—almost two grand! That takes talent, you know. You have to know just how to get them to come across."

"You called me about a robbery, Mr. Traynor," you say wearily.

"Oh, yes. Let's see. I got back here a little after eleven. I put my attaché case with the money in it on the bed, and went in to shave. I was standing in front of the washstand, shaving, when I thought I heard a noise behind me. Before I could turn around, I got a terrific blow on my head! I blacked out. When I came to, my attaché case was gone."

"How do you suppose the robber got in?" you ask.

"It had to be through the window that opens onto the fire escape. It was wide open—and I know for sure I didn't open it when I came home."

You look at the bruise on the back of Traynor's head, then walk over to the window and look out through the screen at the fire escape. "Anything else you can tell me?" you ask.

"No—oh, of course some of the other employees at the office knew I was out on collections tonight, and maybe—"

"And maybe nothing!" you say. "*You* took that money—where is it?"

Why do you suspect Traynor?

If Traynor was in front of the washstand shaving when he was struck, he should have been able to see the "intruder" in the mirror in front of him. Also, it is odd that a man with a very heavy beard would be shaving at night instead of in the morning. Furthermore, he said the "intruder" must have entered and left through the window—but it is screened.

33

The Case of the Moonlight Drowning

When you arrive at the resort, it is late in a beautiful evening. The full moon, flooding the surface of the lake with light, shines on a tragic scene. Two men crouch over the drenched body of pretty Doris Fallon. They administer artificial respiration until one of them, John Sykes, shakes his head sadly and says, "Too late—much too late."

The other man, Phil Nash, speaks: "We heard Tom's cries for help." Tom Kenton is the young man standing nearby, looking miserable with sorrow. "So we ran down to the lake. He was just beaching his canoe, and he told us about capsizing 50 feet out on the lake. His girl friend, he said, was still out there."

"What did you do?"

"We searched from our motorboat," Sykes says. "Then John here found the girl under the water. But it was too late!"

You look questioningly at young Tom Kenton.

"It happened so suddenly!" he exclaims. "Doris and I were out there in the canoe, having a wonderful time. Then she decided to change seats. All of a sudden we tipped over and were thrown into the water."

"Can you swim?" you ask.

"No, I can't do a thing in the water, and I knew Doris couldn't either. But I managed to hold onto the capsized canoe, while I looked everywhere for Doris. I could hear her pitiful cries for help—but I couldn't see her in the dark. I felt so helpless! Finally I righted the canoe, climbed back in, and paddled back to get help. Oh, I feel awful—I've made such a mess of things!"

"You're right," you say, "you've made a mess of things—including the story you've been telling me. I want you to tell me what really happened."

Why are you suspicious of Tom Kenton's story?

requires a good deal of ability in the water.

struggling girl, the moon has been flooding the lake with light
tonight. Also, despite Tom's claims to helplessness in the water,
he managed to right a capsized canoe and climb into it—which
Although Kenton said it was too dark on the lake to find the

The Case of the Motel Murder

The motel manager takes you to the room occupied by a well-known gambler, Jack Hughes, and opens the door with his pass-key.

You see Hughes' body sprawled facedown across the bed, a knife sticking out from his back. You note the empty quart bottle of whiskey on the bedside table, and a crumpled sheet of note-paper on the floor. You smooth it out and read: "Settle with me now, or else. Smitty."

A young man in a dressing gown enters the room. "I'm Steve Garrison," he says, "the one who found Jack like this. He and I, and Phil Smith, have been in business together for the past year. There's been some bad feeling between Jack and Smitty lately, but I never dreamed that. . . ." He shakes his head.

"Tell me what happened," you say.

"Well, my room is a couple of doors down the hall. This morning I came out to the hall to pick up the paper outside my door. I saw the bellboy knocking at Jack's door, with a bottle of whiskey on a tray. Jack opened the door, took the bottle, tipped the boy, and slammed the door shut again. I went back to my room and looked at the headlines for a few minutes. Then I decided to see Jack about a business matter. I opened his door and saw him— lying on the bed with a knife in his back!"

"Does Smith live here too?" you ask.

"No," Garrison says. "He has a flat in town."

35

You think for a moment. Then you turn to Garrison, the manager, and the bellboy, who are standing together near the door. You ask, "Has anyone touched or moved anything in the room since the body was discovered?"

All three shake their heads. Pointing a finger dramatically at one of them, you say, "You're my suspect!"

Whom did you point your finger at, and why?

Steve Garrison. Although the manager had to use his passkey to open Hughes' door, Garrison said he had walked right in to discover the body. He also attempted to direct your suspicions to Phil Smith, though he shouldn't have known about the note signed "Smitty." And how could the now empty bottle of whiskey have been delivered *and* consumed in a "few minutes?"

The Case of the Mugged Medic

"I've been mugged!" shouts the speaker on the phone. "You'd think that being a physician would entitle me to some consideration!"

You ask him for the story.

"I'm Dr. Henry Harrison. I was on my way to the hospital, when a young hoodlum pulled a knife on me!"

"What did he take?" you ask.

"My solid-gold watch and my wallet, with $150 in it. I even told him I was a doctor, on my way to an emergency, but do you think that did any good?"

"Give me a description," you say. He does. "Don't worry—we'll catch him," you say. "Be in my office at noon tomorrow."

Noon arrives, and so does Dr. Henry Harrison. He rushes in, visibly agitated.

"I've lined up two possibilities," you say. "They haven't been told why they were picked up. Watch and listen carefully while I question them."

The first boy, Ted Lawrence, is brought in. He is thin, with long, dark hair, and a leather jacket. "What's happening?" he asks angrily. "There I was, doing nothing, when I get taken for a ride."

You look at Dr. Harrison. He says, "Well, it could be him. But it was quite dark."

"Hey, come off it, Doc!" the boy shouts. "It wasn't me!"

The second boy is brought in. Danny Cahill looks very much like Ted Lawrence—same jacket, same hair.

"What—what's going on?" he sputters. "I didn't do nothing! You can't do this to me!"

You look at the doctor again. "I can't be sure," he says.

"But *I* can," you say. "The guilty boy convicted himself."

Who is guilty? How do you know?

Ted Lawrence is guilty. In the office, the boys were never told that Harrison was a doctor. However, Harrison had told the mugger. Ted Lawrence showed he was guilty when he addressed Harrison in the office as "Doc."

The Case of the Murdered Matron

"She was stabbed to death in her own bed!" the elderly house-keeper cries.

"There, there, Miss Farmer," you say, from across your desk. "Tell me all about it."

Adelaide Farmer shoots a glance at Milton Brown, Mrs. Herman's attorney, and then continues. "My relationship with Mrs. Herman was always of the best. I was more like family than a servant. And my salary was very good."

"However," you say, "you two were the last people to see her alive. And, since she had no family, and you are both to share in her estate—you are both my chief suspects!"

They are shocked and indignant.

"Miss Farmer," you say, "tell me what happened last night."

"Well," she says, "I was cleaning the kitchen when Mr. Brown here left the house, about 7 o'clock last night. Fifteen minutes later I went up to my room, which is next to Mrs. Herman's. Not a sound did I hear from her room, so I thought she'd gone to bed earlier than usual. In the morning her alarm clock woke me at 7:30. It's a very loud one, you know. I went downstairs to prepare her breakfast on a tray, brought it to her room, and found her there, lying on the bed, dead—with a horrible knife in her back!"

You turn to Mr. Brown. "What was the purpose of your visit last night?" you ask.

"Legal matters," he replies brusquely. "And I certainly left her alive and in good health!"

"I wouldn't be too sure of that!" yells Miss Farmer.

You break in. "I was sure from the first it was one of you. Now I know which one!"

Whom do you suspect, and why?

You suspect Adelaide Farmer. She said that Brown left the house at 7:00 last night and that Mrs. Herman's alarm rang at 7:30 this morning. If Brown had killed Mrs. Herman before he left, the alarm would either have gone off at 7:30 *that evening* (if it had been set), or it would not have gone off at all the next morning. Mrs. Herman must have set the clock after 7:30 last night, and was killed some time after that. (The clock was an old-fashioned one that would ring at every 7:30, morning or evening.)

The Case of the Room-mate's Remains

You drive to an old boardinghouse near the university and knock on the door of a room on the second floor. Jerry Morgan, who lets you in, phoned you 20 minutes ago. His room-mate, Tom Hart, lies on the floor, with a switchblade sticking out of his chest.

You check the body. Hart has obviously been dead for several hours. Near the body is a chair on which two raincoats have been carelessly thrown. In the pockets of the topmost raincoat, you find a .38 caliber gun.

"That's mine," Morgan says. "I have a license."

You examine the other raincoat and find only a pair of leather gloves and an empty liquor flask. You ask Morgan for his story.

"I sacked out early last night," he says. "About 10:30, I guess, and I fell asleep right away. Then I was suddenly awakened. All the lights were on, and Tom was stumbling around the room. I hadn't seen him all evening, but he must've been doing some heavy drinking. He was pretty far gone.

"Well, I told him to take it easy and go to bed. After a lot of fumbling, he managed to get his raincoat off and throw it on the chair. Then he fell into bed. I fell asleep again too. When I woke up this morning about seven, there he was on the floor—with that knife stuck in him!

"Somebody must've come in during the night—maybe one of those gambler friends of his. You know, he told me once that he'd been losing a lot, and he gave out some IOU's that he didn't think he could make good. Anyway, as soon as I recovered from the shock, I phoned you."

"Did you disturb or touch anything here before or after phoning me?" you ask.

"Oh, no. I've read enough detective stories to know better than to do that."

"In fact," you say, "I think you know more about this murder than you've told me. I want you to start telling me the truth!"

What part of Morgan's story has made you suspicious?

Morgan said that after Tom Hart woke him up, he threw his raincoat on the chair and fell into bed—and that he, Morgan, had disturbed nothing. Yet you found Morgan's coat lying *on top of* Hart's.

The Case of the Slaughtered Student

A young college student, Tom Allison, was clubbed to death late this evening. He was found in the school's arts-and-crafts room, which he was the only one to use tonight. You have learned that Tom started a new hobby this evening, assembling model cars. You see his first half-completed car on the work table, spattered with blood.

So far, two young men seem to have possible motives. A week ago, Allison turned in a report to one of the deans of the college about the dope-selling activities of a group of students. These students were put on probation and their two leaders were heard making threats to "get even" with Allison.

You call on one of them, Fred Baker, who does not show any reaction to news of the crime. "So someone clobbered him to death," he says. "Big deal. You can't try to pin it on me!"

"Cool down," you say. "I'm just after the facts. How well did you know Tom Allison?"

"Hardly at all. Okay, so I stopped him on the campus this past week—to tell him what I thought of his running to the dean about us. I told him to stick to his little model cars."

"Well, Baker," you say. "You're coming to headquarters with me on suspicion of murdering Tom Allison!"

Why do you suspect Fred Baker?

Tom Allison started his model-car hobby on the night he was murdered. Since he was the only one who used the arts-and-crafts room that night, only the killer would know about his model cars. Fred Baker's mention of model cars—as though Allison had been making them for some time—has made you suspicious of him.

The Case of the Smug Student

You sit at your desk. Donald Martin, arrogance showing all over his face like a bad case of measles, thrusts a piece of paper at you. You read: "Donald Martin: You have always talked entirely too much for your own good. Now, very soon, doom will strike you!" Typewritten and anonymous, of course.

"It's definitely a threat, isn't it?" Martin asks. "You really have to be sick to do this kind of thing, don't you? And I know just the pitiful slob who would do it—my math professor, Dr. Amos Tucker!"

"Why do you suspect him?" you ask.

"He's supposed to be a mathematical genius, but I think he's just a crackpot! I know more about his own subject than he does, and he knows it too! A couple of times I showed him up in front of the whole class. Everyone knew he was wrong and I was right! But to sink so low—to send anonymous letters!"

You watch the conceited young man, thinking that if anyone deserved to be threatened . . . but it's your duty to investigate. "I'll look into it," you say.

Night comes, and you're knocking on the professor's door. He conducts you to his study. "What can I do for you?" he asks. "Something to do with my work perhaps?"

You say, almost apologetically, "I'm investigating a letter received today by one of your students, Donald Martin. This letter—"

The mild-mannered professor becomes a raging fury. "It's about time someone threatened that swell-headed young beast! Maybe this will teach him a lesson."

"Maybe so," you nod. "And I'm inclined to agree with you that he needs teaching. But not with your methods. Threatening letters are an improper solution to *any* problem, Dr. Tucker!"

How do you know Dr. Tucker sent the letter?

Before you had even said what sort of letter it was, Dr. Tucker broke in, implying the letter was a threat.

The Case of the Soft-Drink Stand

You are examining the body of Tom Simms, who ran the soft-drink concession at the county fairgrounds. The blood-encrusted wound over his left temple shows the cause of his death, but a search of the area has not revealed the weapon.

Two men stand nearby: Frank Mason, general manager of the fairgrounds, and Jim Jenkins, the worker who discovered the body.

"It was around midnight," Jenkins says. "Most of the people were gone for the night. I was walking near Tom's place here, and I saw some guy bent over this body on the ground."

"Did you get a good look at the other man?" you ask.

"It was too dark, and when I started toward him, he took off in a hurry. Then I saw Tom was dead, so I ran to Mr. Mason's office and told him about it."

"Poor old Tom," Frank Mason says. "I'd been talking to him only about an hour earlier. He said he'd had a good night's business—over $300. It's gone, by the way—I checked his cash drawer. Someone must have overheard Tom telling me about the money—he had a loud voice."

Mason pauses to light the cigar stub clenched between his teeth. He goes on, "It was quite a shock when Jenkins tore into my office with the news that Tom had been slugged over the head with one of his own empty soft-drink bottles!"

"Here's another shock for you," you say. "I'm taking Jenkins to headquarters for further questioning about this murder!"

What makes you suspect Jenkins?

Although you could not find a weapon near the scene of the crime, Jenkins showed his possible guilt when, according to Mason, he ran into Mason's office with the news that Tom Simms had been slugged with a soft-drink bottle.

The Case of the Stolen Formula

Roger McLaren is telling you his story. "My company has been developing a new formula, and I've been one of the chief people assigned to it. This evening I was working on it in the laboratory, when I left my desk and went behind the partition at the end of the room for a drink of water.

"All of a sudden I heard a suspicious sound. I peeked through the crack in the partition and saw a man with a gun rummaging through my desk. I didn't dare look too long. I used the phone back there to quietly dial the police and explain what was happening to the sergeant who answered."

"And the thief got most of the formula?" you ask.

"Yes. And it's valuable. My company has received some big offers for it. I've even been approached secretly by some unscrupulous outfits who tried to get me to give them the formula for a very attractive price."

"Can you describe the thief?"

"Well," McLaren says readily, "he was a shade under 6 feet tall, weighed about 180 pounds, brownish hair, ruddy complexion. There was a small scar on the back of his left hand."

"Was anyone else working in the building this evening?"

"Only the elevator man, and he already told me he didn't see anyone. Of course, the thief could easily have slipped in and used the stairway without being seen."

"I don't think it happened that way," you say. "I suspect you fell prey to an attractive offer from one of those 'unscrupulous outfits.'"

Why do you suspect this?

Since only a partition separated McLaren from the "thief," you can't see how he could dial the telephone and speak with the police sergeant without being overheard by the intruder. Furthermore, he first told you he didn't dare look too long at the intruder—then, in his enthusiasm for his story, he gave a complete description of the man.

The Case of the Strangled Owner

After getting a frantic phone call, you hurry to the Adams Auto Company. When you enter the repair shop, a young man in grease-covered shirt and trousers comes to meet you. He wipes off his blackened hands, grips your hand tightly, and says, "I'm Terry Conway. Over there—it's Mr. Adams."

You walk farther back into the shop and look at the well-dressed body of Walter Adams. Judging from the ugly dark bruises on his throat, you assume that he has been strangled. You see the open switchblade clutched in his right hand, and you note the fact that there are no cuts, marks, or bruises anywhere except on his throat.

Terry Conway slumps down on a stool and buries his face in his hands. "I didn't mean to do it," he says. "It was a terrible accident."

"Tell me the story," you say.

"This afternoon Mr. Adams came back here from the showroom to tell me I had to work overtime. I told him I couldn't stay tonight—my wife's expecting me home for a special dinner party. Anyway, Mr. Adams was asking me to work overtime too much lately. He got real ugly about it this time. I saw this crazy look in his eyes."

"You argued?"

"Yes. Then he whipped out that knife and came for me. I grabbed the hand he was holding the knife in. Somehow I got him by the neck with my other hand. We struggled all over the place for several minutes, and I guess I must have been squeezing pretty hard on his neck.

"All of a sudden he slumped down on the floor—dead! But I swear it was self-defense!"

You walk around the repair shop and notice the signs of a fight: oil drums tipped over, a board of tools from the wall lying on the floor.

Finally you say, "I'm not too sure this was self-defense. It looks like murder to me."

Why do you suspect murder?

44

If Conway had struggled with Adams, as he said, and had held his right hand with one hand and his throat with the other, there would have to be some grease or dirt on Adams' throat and hand, and perhaps some bruises on his hand. But you found no marks or bruises except on his throat.

The Case of the Suburban Safecracker

You and John Hale are in the yard of his lavish suburban home. An expensive little sports car roars into the driveway, skids to a stop, and Hale's son, Tom, climbs out.

"Where were you this morning at the time of the robbery?" you ask him.

Tom Hale looks evenly at you. "Me? I've been putting my car through its paces for the past couple of hours—getting it ready for the big rally."

"Mr. Hale," you say to the father, "let's go over it again."

"I told you everything," Hale says. "After shaving in the upstairs bathroom, I came down to my study. I found the wall safe wide open, and $3,000 in cash gone. All of my wife's jewels too. Of course, I'm insured, so I won't lose much. But I'd like to throttle the scoundrel who did it!"

"Guess I'll have to wait a while for that loan I asked you for last night—huh, Dad?" Tom asks.

His father gives him a stony, impatient look.

"What about your household staff?" you ask.

Hale replies, "Well, my cook's been at her sister's home 50 miles away since last night; today's her day off. My yard man has been in town all morning, buying supplies. I gave him some money from the safe this morning, so I know the $3,000 was still in there. My chauffeur has spent the morning washing the cars in the garage.

"Well," Tom says to you lightly, "good luck in catching the crook!"

"Thank you," you answer politely, "but my 'good luck' is your *bad* luck. You're under suspicion of robbery!"

Why do you suspect Tom?

Tom didn't ask any questions, or even act surprised, when you asked him where he was at the time of the robbery. If he had been out in his sports car, as he claimed, he would have known nothing about the robbery.

The Case of the Suspicious Suicide

The body lies sprawled in the easy chair next to the window in the hotel room.

Harry Cosgrove phoned you about it. "Tom Hayes was one of my best friends," says Cosgrove. "He shot himself right here, in front of me! I knew that he'd been ill the past few months. But he was always a cheerful person, and I never dreamed that he would. . . ."

You stoop beside the corpse. There is scorched hair around the bullet hole in the right temple, showing the close range from which the shot was fired. Then, stepping around in front of the body, you pick up the gun from the floor with your handkerchief. You give it the fingerprint test and find nothing.

You turn to Cosgrove again. "You say it all happened right in front of you?"

"Yes. I was visiting him and we were talking about nothing in particular. Suddenly he got up from that chair, went to the dresser, pulled the gun out of a drawer, and shot himself!"

You walk across the room to the dresser, look down at the still-open drawer, and stride back to the body for a final check.

"You know, Cosgrove," you say, "I happen to know that Tom

46

Hayes had loaned a lot of money to various friends. And you were his biggest debtor. I think you figured rubbing out Hayes was easier than rubbing out your debt!"

Why do you suspect Cosgrove of murder?

First, although Hayes' bullet wound is in the right temple, you found the gun lying on the floor to the *left* of his chair. Next, you found no fingerprints at all on the gun—pure stupidity on the part of the killer, who wiped the gun clean and forgot to put Hayes' prints on the gun! Also, the dresser from which Hayes supposedly got the gun was quite a distance from where he had "shot himself." An innocent Cosgrove ought to have had time to stop his friend before he walked back to the chair to shoot himself.

The Case of the Telltale Typing

The body of the victim has been examined, photographed, and taken to the morgue. You and Lt. Anderson are left in the small office of writer Adam Evans. Lt. Anderson says, "Adam was a specialist in crime stories, you know. He also specialized in gambling away his earnings and welching on his debts."

You say, "He must've welched on one debt too many—and died for it. According to his landlady, only two men called on him today—Joe Albers and Buzz Stuart—and both of them run gambling houses that Evans was known to visit."

Lt. Anderson says, "I already questioned them. Both admit that Evans owed them money. And they both admit coming here this afternoon, but they each said Evans already had the knife in him when they got here."

You take another look at the sheet of paper in Evan's typewriter, with the strange line of typing:

u93 qog34s i8oo3e j3

"I think Evans typed out his killer's name," you say. "The doctor said he might have lived a couple of minutes after the knife

47

went in. And when a dying man drags himself across a room—as he must have, judging from the trail of blood on the carpet—just. to get to his typewriter, he *must* be trying to leave a message!"

You study the message for several minutes. Then you snap your fingers, sit down at the typewriter, and type out the message that Evans intended to leave.

Who killed Evans? How did you figure it out?

Joe Albers was the murderer. In touch-typing the eight fingers are put on the "home row" of keys before any typing is done—the letters a-s-d-f for the left hand, and j-k-l for the right hand. From these positions the fingers reach out automatically for the other letters. You have realized that Evans, in his weakened condition, must have started typing with his fingers on the wrong row of keys. By working one row higher, you work out the message: "joe albers killed me."

The Case of the Tin Box Theft

"Losing $150 isn't so bad," says Roger Cline. "I'm covered by insurance. But learning that one of my employees may be a thief—*that's* bad!"

You're in Cline's real estate office in response to his phone call. He told you that he usually kept about $150 in a tin box in a desk drawer, under some ledgers. He had been sure that none of his employees even knew about this money, which he used when he ran out of personal cash.

He returned to his office today after lunch and found the money gone. "I haven't told any of my people about this yet," Cline says.

You go into the outer office, where the three employees are: Bill Fergus, a salesman; Betty Carter, a stenographer; and Mary Masters, a clerk. You introduce yourself and say: "Mr. Cline is missing a sizeable sum of money from his office. I must question you three first, since you all have access to the private office. Afterwards, we can check out the building employees and outside callers."

Bill Fergus is indignant. "Well, I only go into his office when he's there! We discuss business out here at my desk. And why would I be digging under the ledgers in his desk drawer?"

"I've been working here for three years," says Betty Carter. "Mr. Cline pays me a generous salary, and I'd never dream of stealing from him!"

"I can't agree about the 'generous salary'," says Mary Masters. "I'm just able to make ends meet. But to take a chance on stealing—oh, no! You better talk to some of the cleaning women, or maybe the window washers, but not *us!*"

"Thank you for the advice," you tell her. "But I'm afraid the thief *is* one of you!"

Which one do you suspect, and why?

Bill Fergus. He said he wouldn't be "digging" under the ledgers" in Cline's desk drawer. Cline had told you he was sure none of his employees knew about the money, and you had not mentioned where the money had been hidden.

The Case of the Trespassing Tramp

Warren Eaton strides off the patio of his country home as you park your car in the driveway.

"I must thank you for coming," he says. "This is definitely a most annoying circumstance."

You follow him along a gravel path to the wooded area of his estate. "A lot of trespassers come through these woods," Eaton says. "I don't like to see these bums littering the area. I warned this particular fellow several times to get out—and I thought that he had gone for good. But evidently he hadn't—and now the worthless creature is dead."

You arrive at the dusty bank of a little pond. At the side of the water, wearing filthy, dust-covered clothes, lies the body of a man. His straggly hair is water-soaked, and his stubbly face is covered with mud. You notice that he is not wearing any socks, and that one of his dusty shoes is missing a shoelace.

"How was he found?" you ask.

"I was walking along here about 20 minutes ago and found him floating facedown in the pond, close to the edge. I quickly pulled him out, but I could tell right away that he was beyond needing artificial respiration. So I hurried back to the house and called your headquarters."

"What about your sleeves—getting soaked to the elbows like that?" you ask.

"When I reached in to pull him out," Eaton says. "You know, I suppose he had a heart attack. Of course, I knew him only from telling him several times that I'd call the police if he didn't stay off my land. But I noticed that his health looked bad—bad enough for his heart to fail when he was bending over the pond for a drink of water."

"A very interesting theory," you say. "However, I suspect that he was murdered—and that you know something about it!"

What makes you suspicious of Warren Eaton's story?

If Eaton had found the man's body floating in the pond, the victim's clothes would have been wet—not dusty, as you found them, with only his hair wet and his face muddy. Eaton's heart-attack theory is too pat a story, and his wet sleeves lead you to suspect he might have stolen up behind the man while he was drinking from the pond, and held his head under the water until he drowned.

The Case of the Well-Dressed Thief

Bob Harkness is the manager of the Eat-Well Supermarket. You go to see him when he reports the robbery of more than $7,000 of the store's receipts.

"He was a big, tall fellow," Harkness says. "I couldn't see much of his face—he had a broad-brimmed brown felt hat pulled down over his eyes. His brown overcoat was buttoned up to the neck, with the collar up and covering the lower part of his face."

"How did it happen?" you ask.

"I was sitting here at my desk, adding up the day's receipts. Suddenly I heard this voice behind me telling me to put up my hands. I glanced back and saw him standing just inside the door with a gun in his hand. He told me to get up from the desk and stand against the wall. Then he scooped all the money from the desk into a black briefcase."

"What then?" you ask.

"He ordered me back to the chair, and he pulled a rope out of his pocket, tied me to the chair, stuffed a big handkerchief in my mouth, and slipped out the door. It took me around 10 minutes to work myself loose from the rope—then I phoned your headquarters."

"Anything else about the robber that can help us identify him?"

"Well," Harkness says, "he spoke with an almost pleasant manner, in a very nice voice. He was well-dressed, too—clean white shirt, blue paisley tie. Oh, this may help you: he had on a tie-clip with an initial . . . let's see, it was an 'F'."

"Tell me," you ask, "is the supermarket insured against this loss?"

"Oh, sure. They won't be losing anything."

"But they will," you say. "They'll be losing a manager! I think you framed this robbery yourself!"

What has led you to this conclusion?

Harkness told you originally that the robber's overcoat was buttoned up to the neck, with the collar up. Then later—in his eagerness to divert suspicion from himself—he described the robber's shirt, tie, and tie-clip. Yet he could not have seen these items under a buttoned-up coat.

The Case of the Woodpile Burial

You're on your way to the scene of the crime. You have company, an unsavory character named Mike Mullen. "Gus hid the body under the woodpile," Mike says. "But, say, you got to promise to keep me out of this." He looks a bit worried.

"Okay," you say. You park in front of a weather-beaten shack with a huge woodpile next to it. "Let's hear the story again," you say.

"Okay." Mullen scratches his chest. "Well, Gus and Sam were havin' it out there in front of the door when I got back. We all of us sacked out here last night. I got up early to stretch my legs a little. When I got back, they were fightin' so hard, they didn't even see me. That suited me just fine—I didn't want nothin' to do with their beef. So I got behind the bushes and watched them from a good safe spot!"

"What did you see?"

"Gus picked up a log and smashed it down on Sam's head! Sam looked deader 'n a doornail. Then Gus started looking around, so I beat it out of there as fast as I could! I got clear to town without stoppin' once, and then I called you."

With Mullen's help, you dig the body out of the woodpile. Not very pretty. Crushed skull, plenty of blood, and brains almost spilling out.

"What about last night?" you ask Mullen. "Any trouble between them?"

"Nope. Of course, they was both always kind of touchy and hot-tempered. But I never would've figured on Gus doin' this!"

"Well, I suspect your figuring was right, pal," you say. "Gus didn't—*you* did!"

Why do you suspect Mullen?

Mullen told you the body was buried under the woodpile. If he had left right after the fight, as he said he did, then he could not have known where the body was hidden.